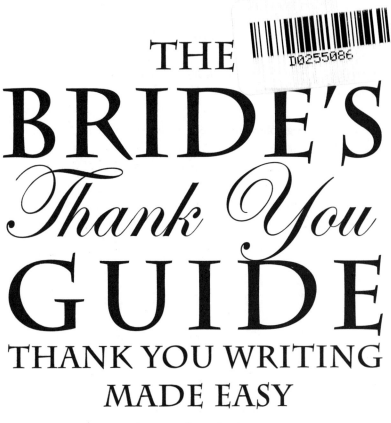

THE
BRIDE'S
Thank You
GUIDE
THANK YOU WRITING
MADE EASY
Second Edition

Pamela A. Lach

CHICAGO
REVIEW
PRESS

Library of Congress Cataloging-in-Publication Data
Lach, Pamela A., 1954-
    The Bride's thank-you guide : thank-you writing made easy / Pamela A.
Lach. — 2nd ed.
        p. cm.
    Includes bibliographical references and index.
    ISBN 978-1-56976-283-7 (pbk.)
    1. Thank-you notes. 2. Wedding etiquette. I. Title.

BJ2092.P55 2010
395.4—dc22

                                                                2009034842

A variety of names have been used for the purpose of providing
examples. Any similarity to actual people is purely coincidental.

Cover and interior design: Jonathan Hahn
Cover image: Scops / iStockphoto

Second edition
Published by Chicago Review Press, Incorporated
814 North Franklin Street
Chicago, Illinois 60610
ISBN 978-1-56976-283-7
Printed in the United States of America
5 4 3 2 1

Contents

Introduction ≈ *Why You Should Write Thank-You Notes*   v

PART I

Getting Started

List of Questions   3
1 ≈ Your First Questions Answered   7
2 ≈ Make It Easy: Use a System   13
3 ≈ Stationery   17

PART II

Writing the Note

4 ≈ General Outline   25
5 ≈ Special Situations   33

PART III
Sample Letters

List of Sample Letters for Those Who Helped 41

6 ⁓ Sample Letters for Those Who Helped 43

List of Sample Letters for Gifts Received 59

7 ⁓ Sample Letters for Gifts Received 61

Resources 77

Gift Ideas 77

Web Sites 82

Index 85

Introduction

Why You Should Write Thank-You Notes

Your wedding has come and gone, and it was one of the most memorable events of your life. You received many wonderful gifts. Other people went out of their way to help. Now it is time to let them know you are grateful. You probably aren't looking forward to it. Whether you have 50 notes to write or 500, the task still looms ahead.

Perhaps you are looking for a way out. "Why should I write all those notes?" you ask. "Everyone knows I'm grateful. If they really cared about me, they wouldn't expect me to spend all my time writing these notes."

After all, what would happen if you didn't write them? You already have the gifts—they can't take them back. People would still speak to you; they wouldn't end a friendship or disown you over a thank-you note (unless they were really stuffy). So why bother?

If your thinking has gone that far, it's time to ask yourself, "Why did they bother?" Coworkers, friends, relatives, and neighbors helped to share in one of the biggest celebrations of your life— your wedding. They may have watched you grow up or shared your excitement as you became engaged and made the wedding plans. When the time came, they went to your wedding and perhaps to other parties given for you before the big day. To celebrate the occasion properly, they may have gone out and bought special clothes, gotten new haircuts or hairstyles, had their nails done, taken time off work, or hired babysitters.

Buying the gift required time and effort. They may have spent hours, even days, poring over your wedding registry, then used their lunch breaks to run from store to store, searching for that perfect item for you to treasure. For those who gave monetary gifts, it's possible that they stretched their budgets to the limit in order to help you and your partner have a good start on your life together.

In addition to offering gifts, many people went out of their way to make this time in your life a special one. Some hosted showers and parties, some ran extra errands for you or made special arrangements on your behalf, and some contributed financially to the wedding celebration.

They too could have said, "Why bother?" Someone might have justified his or her lack of effort by saying, "I'm too busy. What will happen if I ignore all the wedding hoopla? The world won't end."

I'm sure you see the point. They went through all the trouble and made the effort for you. Now it's time for you to do the same.

Telling them "thanks for everything" (whether in person; by phone, text message, instant message, or e-mail; or through your social networking site or wedding Web site) is not enough. Putting a little card by each plate at the reception is thoughtful, but it isn't enough. Cards with preprinted verses offering your thanks are not enough. Only a personal thank-you note can allow you to fully express your gratitude.

I'm not saying you don't want to tell each person how much you appreciate his or her generosity; I know you do. But I'm trying to make it clear that the best way to do this is the customary way. You must write a personal note of thanks.

This may be a task you're dreading. You might be wondering how you'll find time to write them all. You may feel uncomfortable about how to word each note. You might be concerned that you don't know how to write them "properly."

There are only two real rules. They are (1) that you write them, and (2) that you send them out promptly. What you say in the notes is not as important as the fact that you made the effort—and, in doing so, made a personal gesture.

This book won't make the task go away. However, it will provide you with a lot of helpful ideas that will make the job easier. It will also help you write warm and memorable notes. It offers a general outline of a thank-you note and provides you with the basic structures for different types of notes. There are chapters containing sample words, phrases, and actual letters you can use. Guidelines for the proper etiquette for special situations will also be discussed.

Once you begin to compose your notes you will have two options. You can either pick and choose from the list of words and phrases I have provided and form your own note, or you can refer to the introductory list of sample letters before chapters 6 and 7 and find the one that best matches the gift or situation. Just change the names and use it for your own note.

Because there are many ways of saying thank you, there is also a resources section with gift ideas in the back of the book. You can use it when selecting gifts for your attendants, your spouse, and anyone else who made an extra effort for you during this time.

The thought of writing 50, 100, or 500 notes can overwhelm anyone. You may feel you're saying the same things over and over again. You probably will find it frustrating to try and continually change the wording in your notes. Although you certainly want each note to sound fresh, each guest is only going to read his or her own note. So don't worry too much about repetition.

Finally, take them one at a time. Don't think about the total number—whether it's 50 or 500, just focus on the one in front of you. And with each note you finish, your task will seem easier and easier. Believe me—by the time you write the final note, you will be an expert. And before you know it, they'll be done.

Good luck!

Part 1

Getting Started

List of Questions

1 Your First Questions Answered   7

"Who writes the notes?"   7

"Do we sign both our names?"   7

"Can I sign a note with my married name if I write it before the wedding?"   8

"When do I send the notes?"   8

"What are some ways to save time?"   8

"Whom do I send thank-you notes to?"   9

"Can I send a thank-you note before the wedding?"   9

"What return address should I use if I write the note before the wedding?"   9

"Should I mail them as I write them or wait and send all the notes at the same time?"   9

"Is it enough to thank someone in person?"   10

"Is it okay to e-mail or text my thank-yous?"   10

"We posted a nice thank-you message on our wedding Web site. Isn't that enough?"   10

"We placed little scrolls with preprinted thank-you verses next to each plate at the reception. Isn't that enough?"   10

*"We sent out preprinted acknowledgment cards
as we received a gift. Isn't that enough?"*   11

*"We bought nice cards with preprinted verses
to sign and mail. Isn't that enough?"*   11

*"I plan to type each personal note on the
computer and then print them onto some
nice paper. What's wrong with that?"*   11

2 ⤳ Make It Easy: Use a System   13

*"How can I be sure to thank the right person
for each gift?"*   13

*"I didn't keep up with my organizer. How do I
know that I've thanked everyone?"*   15

"What if I can't send out all my notes in four weeks?"   16

3 ⤳ Stationery   17

"What kind of paper should I use for the notes?"   17

"What should I put on the front of the cards?"   18

"Can I put my maiden name on the front of the card?"   19

*"What if I plan to keep my maiden name after the
wedding? How should I write our names then?"*   19

*"My fiancé has promised to help write the notes for
gifts received before the wedding. Shouldn't we just
go ahead and put both our names on the front?"*   20

*"I would like to use a monogram on the front.
What are my options?"*   20

"Should the cover lettering be printed,
thermographed, or engraved?"   21

"What can I do with leftover cards?"   21

5 ⤳ Special Situations   33

"How do we sign our notes?"   33

"How do I thank someone for a monetary gift?"   34

"What do I say about duplicate gifts?"   34

"What is the right way to thank everyone who
went in on a group gift?"   34

"We received a gift without a card. Whom do we thank?" 35

"We received a monetary gift in an unsigned card.
How do we trace the giver so that we can thank
him or her properly?"   35

"What if neither of us knows the person who gave
the gift?"   35

"If the gift arrives broken, should I tell the sender?"   36

"A friend of ours attended the wedding but didn't
give a gift. Should I still write a note?"   36

"My cousin claims she sent a gift. We never received
it. My mom says I still must write a thank-you note.
How am I supposed to do that, since I don't know
what the gift is? Should I do that?"   37

"What happens if the wedding is canceled?"   37

"What should I do if the marriage is annulled?"   37

1

Your First Questions Answered

"Who writes the notes?"

In the past, the bride would write the notes and sign her name. Today, most couples share this responsibility.

Writing the notes can be a pleasant way for the two of you to spend an hour or so together each evening. It will help you relive your wedding memories and give you an opportunity to talk about the ways you can use the gifts you've received.

When you share this experience with your partner, you will find that the task is quickly completed. After you're finished, you will both have more time to spend doing your favorite things.

"Do we sign both our names?"

Yes, most couples today sign their thank-you notes with both names.

"Can I sign a note with my married name if I write it before the wedding?"

No, prior to the wedding you would sign with your maiden name.

"When do I send the notes?"

As soon as possible. If the gift arrives up to one week before the wedding, you should send the note within three weeks of its arrival. If you receive the gift after that, four weeks after the wedding is considered the maximum acceptable amount of time for sending out your notes. (This assumes you went on a honeymoon immediately after the wedding.)

A note that arrives months after the wedding lacks enthusiasm. It is inconsiderate. It leaves the giver wondering if you received the gift (unless you sent an acknowledgment card). Remember, she spent time helping you or selecting your gift. She's not expecting too much when she hopes to hear that you enjoyed what she gave you. It is also easier to write the note if you do it while everything is still fresh in your mind.

"What are some ways to save time?"

If you follow these four suggestions, you'll find that you can speed up the process.

- Address the envelopes for your thank-you notes far in advance of writing them. If you do it at the same time that you write your invitations, you will only have to gather the addresses once.
- As soon as you receive a gift, write a description, such as "a hand-painted vase with intricate floral designs." You can use the description when writing your note.

- Have a system of recording gifts to keep track of names and each item received (see chapter 2 for organizational tips).
- Write your notes as the gifts arrive.

"Whom do I send thank-you notes to?"

Send a note to anyone who gave you a gift, attended a celebration, or went out of his or her way to help. This includes members of the wedding party such as ushers, bridesmaids, ring bearers, and flower girls. People you see every day—including both sets of parents, siblings, or friends—still deserve a note of thanks.

You will send more than one note to just about everyone on your guest list. Each gift deserves its own thank-you note. For example, do not thank someone for both her shower gift and wedding gift in the same note; write separate notes for both gifts.

It doesn't matter how small the gift or favor might have been— you should still send the person a note of gratitude.

"Can I send a thank-you note before the wedding?"

Yes! In fact, it will make the process much easier if you write your note as soon as you receive the gift or favor.

"What return address should I use if I write the note before the wedding?"

Use your current address. If you know the address you will use after the wedding, include that information with your note.

"Should I mail them as I write them or wait and send all the notes at the same time?"

If the gift is received before the wedding, write and mail the note as soon as you receive the gift. After the wedding, you might want to mail all the notes together or in batches.

If you don't mail them together, try to sort and send them in groups that may have contact with one another. Coworkers, neighbors, friends, or close relatives might mention to one another that they received your note. It would be wise to make sure that all members of that group receive their notes at the same time. It may sound like a lot of trouble, but believe me, if you don't mail them at the same time, you'll be hearing, "So-and-so received her thank-you note today and I didn't. Didn't you receive my gift?"

"Is it enough to thank someone in person?"

It's nice to thank a guest in person, but it is not enough. A hand-written note of thanks is a better display of gratitude.

"Is it okay to e-mail or text my thank-yous?"

Not if you are trying to use either as a replacement for a hand-written thank-you note.

"We posted a nice thank-you message on our wedding Web site. Isn't that enough?"

No, that type of message is not personal enough. An individual note, written on stationery by you or your partner, is the right way to thank everyone who helped or gave gifts.

"We placed little scrolls with preprinted thank-you verses next to each plate at the reception. Isn't that enough?"

It is a nice gesture. However, it does not replace the personal touch of a handwritten note that specifically mentions why you are thanking your guests.

*"We sent out preprinted acknowledgment cards as we
received each gift. Isn't that enough?"*

Sending out acknowledgment cards is a great way to let your
guests know that their gifts were received. It eases any concerns
they might have about their delivery. Do acknowledgment cards
replace handwritten thank-you notes, though? No, they are still not
personal, handwritten gestures of gratitude.

*"We bought nice cards with preprinted verses to sign and
mail. Isn't that enough?"*

A card with a catchy preprinted message, using words that seem
more clever than you might write yourself—very tempting! But it
doesn't begin to mean as much as a handwritten note. Think about
it. When you receive a card, what do you really want to read—the
preprinted message or the personal note from the sender?

Even worse are cards with preprinted verses *and* preprinted
signatures. You might think, "Oh, what a great time saver!" The
recipient will think, "What a waste of time and postage. This person
really doesn't care enough to send me a personal note."

*"I plan to type each personal note on the computer and
then print them onto some nice paper. What's wrong
with that?"*

It is not a fitting substitute for a handwritten note. Yes, it is
easier. Yes, other people do it. Neither of those reasons makes it
the right thing to do. The point is that you took the time, in the age
of instantaneous digital communication, to write the note on paper
yourself. That effort is what indicates your genuine gratitude.

2

Make It Easy: Use a System

"How can I be sure to thank the right person for each gift?"

This is where organization is important. Every gift should immediately be tagged in some way. Whether you are using a spreadsheet, an online program, or plain index cards, note the name of the giver (or the names of the givers, if it's a group gift) and the gift as soon as you receive it. Keep your records up-to-date and as organized as possible. It will save you a lot of stress in the long run!

Index Cards

Simple and low-tech, using index cards is a very popular organizational method. Some stationers and gift shops have preprinted cards for this purpose. You can also create your own and design the cards by hand or on a computer. If you organize them in alphabetical order, it will be easier to access each name (though sometimes couples choose to keep the card with the gift until the thank-you note has been written to avoid mistakes).

In many cases you will receive more than one gift from each guest (such as engagement, shower, and wedding gifts), and this method allows you to keep all the details in one place. If someone does a special favor—helps address invitations, throws a shower—you can note it on the back of the card.

Here is an example:

Name: _____

Address: _____

Phone: _____ E-mail: _____

Wedding Invitation Sent? _____ Date Sent: _____

Occasion: _____

Gift: _____

Thank-You Sent? _____ Date Sent: _____

Occasion: _____

Gift: _____

Thank-You Sent? _____ Date Sent: _____

Occasion: _____

Gift: _____

Thank-You Sent? _____ Date Sent: _____

Binder System

Another popular method is a three-ring binder system with tabbed index pages. With this system, every aspect of the wedding is in one place. Your contract with the florist is a few pages away from your guest list; the dinner menu for the reception and copies of your marriage license are safely tucked away. You can use the design from the index card example for everyone on your invitation list. Just to be sure to include the following information:

- Name and address
- Occasion
- Brief description of gift
- Date thank-you note was sent

Add details about the gifts when you record their receipt. It will be easier to write the note when you have time.

Database

There are programs available for purchase or online databases at which you can register (such as BridalTrack.com) that keep all of your data in one place. You can also create your own database in Excel. With this method, it's easy to make changes. If you keep your database current, you can instantly check it if you find yourself asking, "What gift did Mr. Cooper send?" or "Did I send a thank-you to Julia for her shower gift?" You can save the data to a portable drive and carry it everywhere. However, a crash or virus could be a disaster if your information cannot be retrieved.

"I didn't keep up with my organizer. How do I know that I've thanked everyone?"

Sit down and think about the past year. Who went out of his or her way to help you? Who gave you a shower or party? Make a list of all the names. Don't forget your parents and your wedding party!

If you do forget someone, you will probably hear about it sooner or later. Be sure to send a thank-you note as soon as you learn about the error.

"What if I can't send out all my notes in four weeks?"

When you have a very large wedding (which usually consists of 200 or more guests) or if you plan a long honeymoon, it may not be possible to acknowledge all your gifts within four weeks. In that case, you can send a preprinted card acknowledging the receipt of each gift as it arrives. This lets the giver know that you have safely received the item.

Acknowledgment cards are not a substitute for thank-you notes. They are placeholders, buying you time to write an actual note of thanks. Here is sample wording for a preprinted acknowledgment card:

> We have received your gift. Thank you very much!
> We will be writing a more personal note in a few weeks.
>
> Fondly,
> Nicole Shapiro and Jeremy Meyers

If you are having a large wedding and a long honeymoon, address the envelopes for the acknowledgment cards ahead of time.

Don't ever say, "Well, it's too late to send a thank-you now." It's never too late—it's just more polite to do it quickly.

3

Stationery

"What kind of paper should I use for the notes?"

In most cases your paper will match your wedding stationery. The type of paper and how closely it adheres to tradition reflects your wedding's style. A rich, thick, white vellum paper indicates a traditional, formal wedding. A thin, colorful sheet on recycled cotton paper suggests a more informal affair. The color and style of your notes should match the rest of your wedding stationery as closely as possible.

Least Formal

Blank cards with the words "Thank You" preprinted on the front are sold everywhere, from grocery stores to trendier, upscale paper stores. According to the formal rules of etiquette, these cards would only be used for small, informal weddings. However, many couples prefer to use them regardless.

More Formal

Another option is using cards with your wedding photograph on the front. The inside should be blank for you to add a personalized note. These cards double as a delightful keepsake from your wedding. To save time, select a card that has a slot in which you can slip a picture after the wedding. You can write the note ahead of time and then just add the picture before you mail it.

Most Formal

Traditional notes are written on four-by-five-inch cards. They match your wedding stationery and can be ordered with your invitations.

"What should I put on the front of the cards?"

You have some options for the front of the card. For notes sent before the wedding, the card would have your full name or a monogram of your initials. After the wedding, it would have your name as you plan to use it. If you prefer, you can use both your names. (Using both names is not quite adhering to formal etiquette, yet it is done often enough to make it OK.)

Before the wedding, it might look something like this:

Brianna Nicole Wilkinson

If you are planning to keep your maiden name or hyphenate your and your partner's last names, the card sent after the wedding would offer that information to your friends and family.

Brianna Nicole Wilkinson

Brianna and Austin Yang-Wilkinson

Brianna Wilkinson Yang

Mrs. Austin L. Yang

Brianna and Austin Yang

Mr. & Mrs. Austin L. Yang

"Can I put my maiden name on the front of the card?"

Yes, you would always do that with cards used before the wedding day. If you plan to use your maiden name after the wedding, you could still use the same cards.

"What if I plan to keep my maiden name after the wedding? How should I write our names then?"

You can indicate your preference by having your maiden name on the front of the card. If you don't have your names on the front, you can include that information at the end of your note. For example, your signatures might read:

Sincerely,
Brianna Wilkinson and Austin Yang

"My fiancé has promised to help write the notes for gifts received before the wedding. Shouldn't we just go ahead and put both our names on the front?"

If your name will remain exactly the same, it is an option. Traditionally he would have his own cards with his name on the front. Men have stationery needs too!

Austin L. Yang

"I would like to use a monogram on the front. What are my options?"

There are many different kinds of personal monograms. If you are not married yet, you should use the initials of your first, middle, and last name.

B N W

If you are married and have taken your spouse's name, your personal monogram would be the initials of your first, middle, and new last name.

B N Y

Or you might prefer to use a joint monogram. One option uses your first names and last initial, as shown below:

Brianna
Y
Austin

Another combines both of your initials in a more traditional style.

B Y A

Remember, anything that is sent should indicate your name the day you send the note. Don't presume and use your married name before the wedding.

"Should the cover lettering be printed, thermographed, or engraved?"

Engraved invitations have raised lettering that feels very elegant to the touch. It is still considered the proper choice for very formal weddings. As such, it can be the most expensive choice. However, if you continue to use engraved stationery, it is possible to save on repeat orders. Thermographed and letterpress stationery are similar to engraved stationery but are created through a less-expensive process.

"What can I do with leftover cards?"

If there hasn't been a name change, you can continue to use them as stationery. They are ideal for sending brief notes, accepting or declining invitations, or writing other thank-you notes. They can also be used as informal invitations or as gift enclosure cards.

Part II

Writing the Note

4

General Outline

Write with a blue or black pen. Other colors are harder to read. Try to write as legibly as possible.

Don't use words that make you feel uncomfortable, and don't try and use formal, stilted language. Just be yourself. You want whoever is reading the note to hear your voice in it. A good trick is to try and picture the person you're writing to as you compose the note. It will make it easier to address that person in the same way you usually do.

The note doesn't have to be long—only a few brief, sincere lines are necessary. The idea is that when the recipient reads it, he feels that you were truly thinking of him. This isn't always easy, especially when you're writing 50 notes at a time. No matter how tired you are, try to make each note sound like it's the only one you're writing.

Start with a note to someone you know well—that makes it easier to get into the flow.

General Outline of a Thank-You Note

The basic structure of each note is as follows:

- Address the person you're thanking.
- Note who is giving thanks (i.e., just you, or you and your partner).
- Thank the person.
- Mention something nice about the gift.
- Tell the person how you might use the gift.
- Make a final pleasant comment.
- Thank the person again.
- Sign off.

In More Detail

Address the Person You're Thanking

If you are writing to a couple, according to tradition, you would address the note to the wife. The husband would then be mentioned in the body of the message. Today, many couples prefer to address the note to both the husband and wife.

The general rule to follow is to address each note with the name you would use when normally greeting that person, whether it is "Mr.," "Auntie," or his or her first name.

If you are writing to your new spouse's relatives, address the note in the same way he or she would.

Dear Mom and Dad,
Dear Mr. and Mrs. Guzman,
Dear Jesse and Julie,
Dear Aunt Monica,
Dear Stephanie,

When you write a note to a large group, you can address it with "Dear friends" or "Dear coworkers" (or whatever most accurately describes the group's relationship to you or your spouse).

Note Who Is Giving Thanks

Identify whom the note is from. For example:

I
Caleb and I
Marissa and I
We

Thank the Person

When you write a lot of notes, you start to run out of ways to say thank you. Here are some different ways to say it:

Aaron and I would like to thank you
Chloe and I are very grateful
We were so delighted when we opened your gift of
Julian and I appreciate
Claire and I were excited to receive
When Mason and I opened your gift, we were thrilled to discover
Kara and I can't thank you enough
I was so pleased

Mention Something Nice About the Gift

It isn't easy to come up with new adjectives and original descriptions for each gift. Remember to mention the gift specifically. Don't just thank him or her for the gift—thank the person for the lovely crystal vase or charming silver tea set. If you aren't sure what the gift is, just describe it. For example, you could say, "Tom and I can't thank you enough for the beautifully carved wooden statue."

Descriptive Words to Borrow

Pick and choose words from this list to keep your notes fresh!

amazing	enjoyable
appealing	etched
appropriate	exquisite
artistic	exotic
attractive	eye-catching
beautiful	fascinating
best	fashionable
charming	glamorous
chic	generous
colorful	gorgeous
considerate	handsome
creative	handy
cute	helpful
dazzling	ideal
decorative	imaginative
delicious	impressive
delightful	interesting
elegant	lavish
embossed	lovely
enchanting	luxurious

magnificent	sophisticated
much-needed	sparkling
opulent	special
perfect	striking
pleasant	stunning
pleasing	superb
practical	thoughtful
pretty	useful
priceless	valuable
remarkable	wonderful

Descriptive Phrases to Borrow

Here are some phrases to help you compose each note:

antique finish	hand-painted
attractive decoration	intricate details
beautifully carved	lifelike details
beautifully crafted	multipurpose
classic style	ornate design
creative pattern	polished brass
delicate design	sculptured pattern
fine embroidery	simple ornamentation
finest quality	sophisticated setting
floral details	swirled glass
future heirloom	unique design

Tell the Person How You Might Use the Gift

No one wants to think that their gift will be tucked away in a closet for the next 20 years. Think about using the item and try to work that into the note. Here are some ideas:

This _____ is such a welcome addition to our collection of _____.

The _____ is perfect for entertaining guests.

We will enjoy using _____ on special occasions.

This _____ will save us so much time because _____.

The _____ really brightens up our _____ room.

This _____ is so versatile, I can't begin to list all the ways we can use it.

I can't believe how well the _____ suits our decor.

The _____ will come in handy when _____.

_____ is a distinctive accessory for our _____.

It is an ideal accent piece for _____.

This _____ will be fun to use when _____.

I can't wait to try _____ the next time we _____.

The _____ will help us to organize _____.

We will always treasure this _____.

Everyone who comes into our home will admire the _____.

The _____ is just what we need for _____.

Make a Final Pleasant Comment

You want to reinforce your gratitude with an extra line.

We will give the _____ a place of honor in our home.

Just knowing how carefully you selected the _____ means so much to both of us.

This _____ is exactly what we wanted.

It means so much to us that you went out of your way to find this _____.

We are so proud to own this _____.

We hope you will visit soon to see how wonderful it looks in our _____.

Thank the Person Again

Thanks to you, _____.
Thanks again for _____.
Again, many thanks for _____.
We can't thank you enough for _____.
I am so grateful that _____.

Sign Off

The words you choose for the closing will depend on your relationship with the addressee. They will match the way you began the note. For example, a note that begins "Dear Mr. and Mrs. Peterson" shouldn't be signed "With love and kisses."

Here are some ideas for concluding your note:

- Affectionately,
- Best regards,
- Cordially,
- Fondly,
- Gratefully,
- Lots of love,
- Love,
- Love always,
- Sincerely,
- Truly yours,
- With affection,
- With appreciation,
- Your friends,

5

Special Situations

"How do we sign our notes?"

Traditionally the bride signs the note. Before the wedding she signs her maiden name; after the wedding, her married name. However, most couples today sign their notes jointly.

Your relationship with the addressee determines how you begin and end the note. You should sign with just your first names *only* if you are positive the recipient will know who you are.

In addition, your signature will offer an indication of how you wish to be addressed after the wedding. Here are some examples:

Sarah and Chad
Sarah Abigail Maguire
Chad Nathan Romero
Mrs. Sarah Romero
Mrs. Chad Romero
Sarah Maguire Romero
Mr. and Mrs. Chad Romero
Sarah Maguire and Chad Romero

"How do I thank someone for a monetary gift?"

Refer to it as "generous" or "thoughtful." Include an explanation of what the money will be used for. You can mention the dollar amount in the note, but you shouldn't share that information with other people.

"What do I say about duplicate gifts?"

No matter how carefully you register your choices, it is almost inevitable that you will receive more than one of the same item at some point. Although there is nothing wrong with exchanging duplicate gifts, it is considered impolite to tell the giver you have done that.

You might receive four sets of wine glasses or two identical picture frames. Even if your guests are aware of the duplication, each wants to believe you would rather keep his or her gift and exchange the other.

Write your note thanking the person for the actual gift they gave you, not what you traded it in for.

"What is the right way to thank everyone who went in on a group gift?"

Sometimes friends or family members like to pool their funds to buy a larger gift. The way you address the note will depend on the number of people who went in together on the gift.

The general rule is that for fewer than six people, each should receive an individual note. Don't make them identical—a word change here and there will make them more personal.

A group note should only be sent to people who are generally found in one place (such as coworkers in an office). The note is addressed to all of them and usually displayed where everyone can read it easily.

"We received a gift without a card. Whom do we thank?"

When cards and gifts get separated, it becomes an adventure in discovering whom to thank for what. First, check with everyone who was with you when you opened the gift. Someone might remember. If that doesn't work, ask both sets of parents and close relatives. The giver might have told one of them about his or her gift. If you still don't have an answer, save this one for last: go through the invitation list and cross off the names of those who you know have given a gift. With any luck, there will only be one name left when you are done. Thank that person for the gift!

"We received a monetary gift in an unsigned card. How do we trace the giver so that we can thank him or her properly?"

This is the hardest type of gift to trace. The only solution is to save it for the end. As with gifts without cards, go through the invitation list and cross off the names of those you have already thanked. If you're lucky, there will only be one name left. If not, write very generic notes to the rest and hope for the best!

"What if neither of us knows the person who gave the gift?"

As long as there is an address, send a thank-you note. If your future spouse and both sets of parents are unclear as to the person's identity, just say thank you for the gift. If the gift was received before the wedding, there is a good chance you'll meet the person at a party or at the wedding. Mention that you are looking forward to seeing him or her at the celebration. Even if the two of you don't meet, it was nice of the person to think of you.

"If the gift arrives broken, should I tell the sender?"

It's a shame when something like this happens. However it's best not to tell the giver that the gift was ruined. It will only disappoint him or her and make that person feel awkward.

If it was shipped directly from the store, you might contact the manager and explain the situation. Some businesses will replace the merchandise. If it was sent through a delivery service, check and see if it was insured. Some companies mark that information clearly on their packaging. Another option is to check the company's Web site. There might be a section on how to file a claim for damaged shipments. Whatever the case, thank the sender for the gift without mentioning its status or condition.

"A friend of ours attended the wedding but didn't give a gift. Should I still write a note?"

According to traditional etiquette, an invited guest has up to 12 months to give a wedding gift. One practical reason behind that tradition is that sometimes the extra cost involved in attending the wedding can make it difficult to purchase a gift as well.

If a guest took the time to take part in your celebration, it is a nice gesture to thank him or her. Gifts are supposed to be a wonderful addition to a guest's presence. If and when you receive a gift from the person at a later date, you should still write a note thanking him or her for the gift. You write a note for both presence and presents!

"My cousin claims she sent a gift. We never received it.
My mom says I still must write a thank-you note. How
am I supposed to do that, since I don't know what the
gift is? Should I do that?"

Things happen; gifts are lost. If you can obtain the shipping information it may be possible to trace it. If not, give her the benefit of the doubt. Perhaps it was stolen. Thank her for whatever she claims to have given you, and you'll keep peace in the family.

"What happens if the wedding is canceled?"
or
"What should I do if the marriage is quickly annulled?"

If the wedding does not take place, all gifts should be returned to those who provided them. The only exceptions would be trivial, inexpensive shower gifts. If the annulment is sought within a few months of the wedding, unused gifts should be returned.

For these situations, you do not have to write an explanation of why or how the circumstances occurred. Just a brief, tactful note is necessary. Each person would write to his or her own friends and family. In the case of gifts from mutual friends, only one of you needs to write a note. There are examples of letters for these situations in part III, the "Sample Letters" section of this book.

Part III

Sample Letters

List of Sample Letters for Those Who Helped

Assisted in some way	43
Best man	44
Bridesmaid	44
Dinner given in your honor	45
Engagement party	46
Floral arrangements	46
Flower girl	46
Groomsman	47
Guest book attendant	47
Hosted wedding guests	48
Maid/matron of honor	48
Music provider	49
New address	49
Officiant	50
Parents (example 1)	50

Parents (example 2)   51
Party given for both of you   51
Party given for just the bride   52
Reader at ceremony   52
Rehearsal dinner   52
Ring bearer   53
Shower given for you (example 1)   53
Shower given for you (example 2)   54
Shower (personal theme)   54
Special favor   55
Usher   55
Videographer   56
Vocalist   56
Wedding consultant   57
Wrote special prayer   57

6

Sample Letters for Those Who Helped

Feel free to use any and all wording from the sample letters in this chapter and the following chapter as your own.

Assisted in some way:

Dear Uncle Ron,

Hailey and I will always be grateful for your generous contribution. Without it, we never would have had the wedding of our dreams. It was so thoughtful of you to offer your assistance as soon as we announced our engagement. You told us then that you wanted our wedding to be the perfect celebration. Thanks to you, it was.

We will never forget how you made it all possible. As we treasure our wedding memories in the years to come, we will always remember how you helped make our dreams come true. Again, thank you.

> With love and affection,
> Devon

Best man:

Dear Connor,

If you ever decide to be a full-time best man, just let me know. I'd be glad to write you a letter of recommendation. I don't think anyone will ever forget my bachelor party—you sure know how to throw one! Thank you for making it a night to remember.

I'll always appreciate the way you organized the groomsmen. You even made sure they knew how to put on their tuxes. It helped to know you had all the details under control. It left me plenty of time to concentrate on being terrified before the ceremony.

Seriously, you were a big help in keeping me calm. Thanks again for being there.

> Your old pal,
> Doug

Bridesmaid:

Dear Sasha,

Will and I were so glad you were able to be such a special part of our wedding. Thank you for all your help and for being there whenever we needed you. We know how busy you are, and we appreciate that you gave up a lot of your time to be such an active member of our wedding party. We want to make sure you know we are incredibly grateful.

I don't know if I would have gotten the invitations addressed without your help. Because you kept the gifts so organized, writing my thank-you notes is incredibly easy. We appreciated the generous check, too. We have picked out a mirror that will hang perfectly in our hallway. Come over and see it sometime!

Thanks again for being such an important part of our wedding celebration. It wouldn't have been the same without you.

Love,
Cassie and Will

Dinner in your honor:

Dear Eric and Sabrina,

Caleb and I want to thank you for the wonderful dinner last night. The food was fantastic—did you really cook it all yourselves? This is such a hectic time for us, so it was nice to relax with good friends. Thank you for caring enough to do this. We know how busy you both are, too. You're the best!

Love,
Kate and Caleb

Engagement party:

> Dear Aunt Rachel,
>
> Thank you for the beautiful party you gave us to celebrate our engagement. It was so nice to gather all our loved ones to share this happy time. Gabe and I will always remember the beautiful dinner, delightful toasts, and special time we had in your new home. Thank you for being so loving, helpful, and supportive. We love you and will keep you posted as we continue to make our wedding plans.
>
> Love and best,
> Gina and Gabe

Floral arrangements:

> Dear Courtney,
>
> Mario and I really appreciate the beautiful job you did overseeing the creation of the floral arrangements for our wedding. It was a wonderful gift of your talents, and you truly outdid yourself. Everything was perfect—from the bouquets to the centerpieces. They look so incredible in the pictures! Your generosity means so much to us. A million thanks! We will never forget all you have done.
>
> With love and affection,
> Elizabeth and Mario

Flower girl:

> Dear Janie,
>
> I'm so glad you were a part of my wedding! You looked so pretty in your long party dress, and you were just like a princess when you walked up the aisle. It was fun to have

you walk ahead of me and drop flower petals. Chris and I think we picked the best flower girl ever to be in our wedding. Thank you for helping create a perfect celebration we will never forget.

Love,
Olivia and Chris

Groomsman:

Dear Luke,

Owen and I know how busy we kept you at our wedding. Thank you for being so patient with us! Between chauffeuring guests, running last-minute errands, and escorting my cousin Mackenzie, you must have been as tired as we were when the day was over.

A million thanks for all that you did. You were a huge help to us and we couldn't have asked for a better groomsman, or a better friend!

Fondly,
Anna and Owen

Guest book attendant:

Dear Theresa,

Thank you for taking the time to make sure our guests signed the register. We wanted to have a record of all our wedding guests and, thanks to you, we will. It was very sweet of you to handle that for us and we appreciate it very much.

Best wishes,
Mia and Alex

Hosted wedding guests:

> Dear Regina and Ben,
>
> We are truly overwhelmed by all you have done for us. We are so grateful to both of you for opening your home to my uncle Mike and cousin Dan. They are still raving about your good cooking, wonderful hospitality, and beautiful yard.
>
> Thank you for the beautiful oil painting, too. What a lovely surprise! It meant so much that you found it for us while you were in Ireland. We have just the right place for it, where everyone will see it as they come into our home.
>
> How did we ever get lucky enough to have you as our friends? Thank you, thank you, thank you! You are the best, and we are so glad to have you in our lives.
>
> Love,
Michelle and Jamal

Maid/matron of honor:

> Dear Lauren,
>
> Did you know what a big job you were taking on when you agreed to be my maid of honor? I am so grateful you agreed to do it, because I don't know what I would have done without your support. You helped me with so many of the hundreds of little decisions I had to make. You gave me a beautiful wedding shower that I will never forget. You calmed my nerves before I left for the church. You fixed my veil when it tore before the reception. Your festive mood inspired our guests as they moved through the receiving line.

You were there for me anytime and every time. You were the best maid of honor that any bride could have. I can't begin to thank you enough for everything. I am so grateful you're my friend!

Love,
Grace

Music provider:

Dear Zach,

Thank you for coordinating the music for our wedding reception. The music you programmed for dancing had everyone on their feet! We appreciate your finding the right equipment and making it all happen. It took a huge load off of our shoulders and was a truly wonderful gift. Thank you for doing so much to help make our wedding reception such a joyous celebration.

With love and gratitude,
Miles and Nicky

New address:

Dear Emma,

Rob and I can't thank you enough for the beautiful clock. It fits perfectly with our decor and will look wonderful in our new living room!

Don't forget that we will be moving on September 30. Our new address will be:

> 4554 Main St.
> Trenton, NJ 08601
> Stop by and see us soon. And thanks again for the perfect clock!
>
> > Your friends,
> > Naomi and Rob

Officiant:

> Dear Reverend Rivera,
> Joshua and I would like to thank you for the lovely service you gave during our wedding ceremony. Both the prayers and sermon were so beautiful. Thank you for helping to make our day very special.
>
> > Fondly,
> > Ava and Joshua Lopez

Parents (example 1):

> Dear Mom and Dad,
> Our wedding was a wonderful celebration and it wouldn't have been possible without your help. Noah and I realize it was not easy for you, yet somehow you found a way to make it very special. We know that so much of it was due to your hard work behind the scenes.
> You are such wonderful parents. Who could be luckier than us? We hope someday that we will be able to repay your loving generosity. Thank you again for everything.
>
> > With love and gratitude,
> > Kay and Noah

Parents (example 2):

> Dear Mom and Dad,
>
> Allison and I want to thank you again for the espresso maker. It was a generous gift on top of everything else you did for us. With two careers and night classes to juggle, I know we'll put it to good use. We are also very grateful for all the help and support you gave us over the last few months. This has been a crazy, hectic time. It was great to know that we could rely on you for practical support and a calming influence.
>
> I hope our marriage will be as loving and enduring as yours has been. You two set a great example and we hope to follow it. Again, thank you a million times over for everything you did for us!
>
> Love,
Emilio and Allison

Party given for both of you:

> Dear Mr. and Mrs. Travers,
>
> Damien and I were so surprised last night! We can't thank you enough for the wonderful evening. How did you manage to keep it so secret?
>
> It is so great to work for a company that cares so much for its employees. We can't wait to see you at the wedding. Thanks again for the unforgettable party!
>
> Best regards,
Sarah Altman and
Damien Reynolds

Party given for just the bride:

> Dear Rachel,
>
> Thank you so much for arranging a luncheon party for me. It was so much fun—and a nice break from all the wedding planning. You certainly know how to treat a friend.
>
> I just loved all the little salads you created. And remember, you promised the secret dressing recipe will be part of my wedding gift. I know Aidan will love it, too. Thanks again!
>
> > Love,
> > Olivia

Reader at ceremony:

> Dear Melissa,
>
> Thank you for being a part of our wedding ceremony. You read beautifully—just the way I hoped the words would sound. I know you were a little nervous, but I couldn't tell at all while you were up there! Thanks again for a great job.
>
> > Fondly,
> > Lindsay

Rehearsal dinner:

> Dear Mom,
>
> Our rehearsal dinner was lovely. It was so nice to spend time with the people we're closest to before the rush of the wedding day took over. Thanks to you, Suzanne and I had

a wonderful time. I know everyone else did, too. You must have spent hours finding just the right location, the nicest atmosphere, and the most delicious menu. We will always appreciate your hard work. It means so much to us that you went out of your way to make it a special night. A big, big thank-you from your grateful son — and future daughter!

Love,

Austin and Suzanne

Ring bearer:

Dear Pete,

    Thank you for doing such a great job as our ring bearer. You made sure we had our rings at the ceremony — you were a very important part of our wedding day! You did a fine job throughout the day and we were so happy that you were a part of our wedding.

With lots of love,

Marie and Jordan

Shower given for you (example 1):

Dear Tabitha,

    Thank you so much for everything. It was a perfect shower — I felt as happy and spoiled as a little kid at Christmas! I know it took many hours of hard work to make it so great. I appreciate it; it means so much to me that I have such a great friend.

Love and best,

Eve

Shower given for you (example 2):

> Dear Shannon,
>
>   Thank you for the wonderful shower. You and Beth did such a beautiful job! You are both so busy; I really appreciate the time and effort that it took from your other interests. Tim was especially impressed by the whole affair. He loved the food and the lighthearted fun. He even complimented the decorations. He claims he had such a good time that he would like to attend every shower I go to from now on.
>
>   We received so many lovely gifts—all thanks to you. You are a great friend, and we will always remember this and so many of the other kind and wonderful things you have done to help us. Thank you for being there for us, for working hard to make our lives easier, and for throwing one heck of a party in our honor.
>
> Your loving friends,
Erin and Tim

Shower (personal theme):

> Dear Claire,
>
>   Thank you so much for the wonderful surprise shower! I was so thrilled to have everyone I'm closest to gathered together. In the chaos of wedding planning, it was nice to have an evening to slow down and just have fun with my closest friends. The food was delicious; the games were a riot. I received plenty of fun items to wear on my honeymoon and many occasions after.

SAMPLE LETTERS FOR THOSE WHO HELPED

I can't tell you how much I appreciate your doing this for me. Thanks a million times over—I'll do the same for you when your day comes!

Love and best,
Candace

Special favor:

Dear James,

I am so grateful you were there for me on my wedding day, especially when things went wrong. When my car wouldn't start, you dropped everything and dashed to the airport to pick up my grandmother. When I picked up the wrong tux, you were there to run it back to the shop and deliver the right one. And when a certain bridesmaid's boyfriend decided to break up with her at our wedding reception, you stepped in and comforted her, danced with her, and helped us avoid a possible catastrophe.

A million thanks for being such a great friend. It meant so much to know that you had my back whenever I needed you most!

Best,
Gavin

Usher:

Dear Ryan,

Thanks for doing such a great job as usher at our wedding ceremony. Several guests complimented us on the dignified way in which you escorted them up the aisle. Jodie and I also appreciate that you left the reception to go back and get the guest book we'd forgotten! I'm glad you're a friend I can always count on. Thanks for everything.

Your friend,

Sam

Videographer:

Dear Ian,

Our wedding film was a priceless gift. We never could have paid for such excellent coverage. We know there had to be some editing time—we remember some embarrassing moments that have managed to disappear from the disk! Thank you so much for creating the perfect record of our wedding memories. We are forever grateful.

With fond affection,

Kelly and Nathan

Vocalist:

Dear Hannah,

We are so grateful for the wonderful gift you gave us on our wedding day. No couple could have asked for a more beautiful song medley at their wedding ceremony. I wish you could have heard all the compliments we received about your singing! You have a wonderful talent. Thank you again and again for making our wedding so special.

With joy and gratitude,

Adrienne and William Chin

Wedding consultant:

Dear Marissa,

Thank you for making my wedding possible. I never knew what a wedding consultant did when we started. I sure do now! There's no way I could have had the wedding I dreamed of without your help. Because of your patience, understanding, superb organizational skills, and dedication to making our day exactly what we wanted, Rick and I had an exquisite wedding celebration. Thank you for making that happen. You truly are doing the right work in your life. You are one in a million!

Best regards,
Deanna Joy Kramer

Wrote special prayer:

Dear Phoebe,

Thank you for the beautiful prayer you offered before we began our wedding dinner. Knowing you wrote it just for us meant so much. It fit the tone of our lives and the mood of the wedding just perfectly. I'm glad you gave us a copy; we plan to have it framed and hang it on our wall so we can treasure it always.

Thanks again for adding an important spiritual touch to our special day.

With affection,
Rose Ford and Mark Quinn

List of Sample Letters for Gifts Received

Bookends	61
Broken gift	62
Cake stand	62
Candles and candleholders	62
Centerpiece bowl	63
Champagne	63
Champagne flutes	64
China place setting	64
Crystal vase	65
Decanter set	65
Digital photo album	65
Exchanged gift	66
Gas grill	66
Gift card	67
Gourmet gift basket	67
Group gift (two of five neighbors)	67

Group gift (to all coworkers) 68
Hand-carved napkin rings 68
Handmade quilt 69
Hand-painted ceramic vase 69
Lace table linens 70
Monetary gift (example 1) 70
Monetary gift (example 2) 71
Monetary gift (example 3) 71
Monetary gift (example 4) 71
Monetary gift (example 5) 72
Musical figurines 72
Not sure what gift is (example 1) 73
Not sure what gift is (example 2) 73
Personal recipe book 73
Returned gift to sender (annulled marriage) 74
Returned gift to sender (broken engagement) 74
Salad serving set 75
Set of picture frames 75
Vintage clock 75

7

Sample Letters for Gifts Received

Bookends:

Dear Mr. and Mrs. Ryan,

We were so delighted when we opened your gift. Dan and I love to read, and these beautiful bookends are a welcome addition to our home. Their tapered design will sturdily prop some of our favorite books, and the green marble offers a lovely accent to our room. Thank you again for selecting something we will both use and enjoy every day. We are looking forward to seeing you at the wedding.

Sincerely,

Liz Doherty and Dan Hayes

Broken gift:

Dear Gina and Derrick,

Thank you for the beautiful crystal pitcher. The intricate design is a delightful fit with our other crystal pieces. Josh and I appreciate your thoughtful choice. I wish I had your talent for selecting such beautiful items.

Fondly,

Emily Goldstein

Cake stand:

Dear Natalie and Becca,

Libby and I both smiled when we opened your gift. You know how I love cake! These stands will literally put each one on a pedestal and keep them fresh under glass. Thank you for thinking of us and for choosing something that both looks great and will be of good use in our everyday lives. We are both really glad you will be at the wedding and are looking forward to seeing you there. Thanks again.

Affectionately,

Steve

Candles and candleholders:

Dear Anne and Scott,

Jackson and I were delighted with your gift. It will really light up our lives. (OK, see what happens when you give us candles?) We both admired the intricate design of the candlesticks and appreciate the nice selection of candles to burn. Thank you so much for selecting this gift for us. We will enjoy them often and think of you as we do.

> Best wishes,
> Taylor and Jackson Becker

Centerpiece bowl:

Dear Mr. and Mrs. Ramirez,

We just love the elegant centerpiece bowl you selected for us. The unique design of leaves that create the base is a work of art. It will add a special flair to our table and we will enjoy using it throughout the year. Thank you for taking the time to find us this special gift. We appreciate your kindness and can't wait to see you at the wedding!

> Sincerely,
> Sonya Nelson and
> Anthony Guzman

Champagne:

Dear Adrian,

Thanks for the bottle of Dom Perignon! John and I were impressed that you thought we deserved it! We decided to save it for a special occasion—our honeymoon. Sharing it will be the perfect way to celebrate our first week of married life. You can be sure that we will savor your gift—and toast you while we enjoy it. Thanks again for thinking of us.

> Affectionately,
> Erica and John

Champagne flutes:

Dear Ms. Rubino,

Thank you so much for the champagne flutes—they are made of the loveliest hand-cut glass I have ever seen. How nice of you to have thought of us while you were in Prague! Adam and I will think of you whenever we enjoy champagne. Thank you for a thoughtful gift we will always treasure.

> Sincerely,
> Nicole Sweeney

China place setting:

Dear Mr. and Mrs. Oshiro,

Trevor and I were delighted to receive a complete place setting of china. Thank you so much—the pattern and style is just what we wanted.

We can't wait to see you at the wedding. Keep your fingers crossed for nice weather—an outdoor wedding is always such a risk. Thank you again for giving us such a lovely and generous gift.

> Best regards,
> Ali Franklin and Trevor Smith

Crystal vase:

Dear Mr. and Mrs. Dunbar,

Thank you for the beautifully etched crystal vase. The butterfly designs are so amazingly detailed! I told Isaac that I'm going to have it filled with brilliant flowers all the time. It has inspired me to plant potted flowers around our patio in hopes of growing a continual supply. Again, many thanks for the lovely gift.

Truly yours,
Katie Williams

Decanter set:

Dear Joan,

Mike and I are dazzled by the decanter set. It has such a gorgeous design, and the crystal is so sparkly that we just love to sit and stare at it. It looks stunning next to the other pieces we have received. You can be sure it will always grace our table when we entertain special guests. You are the greatest—thanks a million!

Your friends,
Tara and Mike

Digital photo album:

Dear Mrs. Lowery,

I've always raved about your special knack for finding the perfect gift. As soon as we opened the box, Jerry knew exactly what I meant. Thank you for the lovely digital photo album. We can't wait to fill it with pictures from our honeymoon!

With gratitude,
Jocelyn Reilly Levinson

Exchanged gift:

Dear Kristen,

We'd both like to thank you for the attractive table lamp. We appreciate the time you must have spent selecting it.

Did you have a good time at the wedding? We didn't get to see much of you, but I hope you enjoyed your evening.

Thanks again!

Sincerely,
Alexis and Brandon Mulligan

Gas grill:

Dear Grandpa,

I learned so much at your side at our family cookouts; they were always such special times. Now you have made it possible for me to continue the tradition by giving us this gas grill. Michelle can't wait to try it out, and we'll invite you for our first outdoor meal! Thanks again for the great gift, and see you soon.

Love,
Dan

Gift card:

> Dear Sarah and Kevin,
>   Thanks for the gift card! It will really come in handy for several home improvement projects—I'm already looking at ideas for bedroom paint colors. Both Mike and I appreciate this thoughtful and helpful gift. Can't wait to see you at the wedding in just a few weeks! Thanks again.
>   Best always,
>   Hailey and Mike

Gourmet gift basket:

> Dear Ross,
>   What a clever gift! We can't wait to sample all the fun items from around the world. Believe me, we love treats—gourmet items are just extra special! The basket is beautiful, too. Once we're done enjoying its contents, I plan to fill it with flowers and enjoy it every day.
>   It was so great to see you at the wedding, and we'll think of you each time we enjoy our gift. Thanks again!
>   With fond affection,
>   Caitlin and Isaac

Group gift (two of five neighbors):

> Dear Mr. and Mrs. Thompson,
>   It was so nice of you and the other neighbors to get together and buy us the elegant silver serving set. What a

special and beautiful gift! It is an instant heirloom that we already treasure. We can't wait to invite you over for tea and serve you from these beautiful items. Thank you again for this lovely gift.

Best always,
Grace and Ryan Rosati

Group gift (to all coworkers):

Dear coworkers,

When we were bragging about our nice patio deck, we never dreamed you would fill it with furniture! Thank you so much, each of you, for this thoughtful and wonderful gift. We will enjoy lounging and eating in the finest style. We'll have to invite all of you over to enjoy it yourselves. You are the best, and I'm so glad you were all there to celebrate our special day. Thanks again for a gift we will use every nice day of the year.

With fond affection,
Lourdes and Rubin

Hand-carved napkin rings:

Dear Mr. and Mrs. Roberts,

Dominic and I just love the beautiful napkin rings. The fact that Mr. Roberts carved them himself makes them even more special. The delicate design and intricate details will make them a showpiece on our dining room table whenever we entertain. They will always have a place of honor in our home.

We were so sorry you couldn't make it to the wedding. We really wanted to thank you in person. Many thanks for your thoughtful creation of this beautiful gift.

Sincerely,

Isabella and Dominic Fox

Handmade quilt:

Dear Nicole,

Thank you for the quilt! I know I could never make one as beautiful as this. The colors are stunning and are a perfect accent in our bedroom. How did you think of such a special design? We are both touched and impressed that you made this for us—we feel that we can't find the right words to tell you how much we appreciate this lovely, thoughtful gift. It will be a treasured heirloom in our family. You are such a wonderful friend. Thanks again and again for this gift.

Love,

Emily and Ian

Hand-painted ceramic vase:

Dear Mrs. Murdock,

Thank you for the hand-painted vase. We love the vibrant colors and lifelike details. We will have it in a place of honor in our apartment and will always treasure this

thoughtful, beautiful gift. Thanks for choosing it for us. We
can't wait to see you at the wedding!

Best wishes,

Joanna Meyers and Ed Patel

Lace table linens:

Dear Mrs. Smith,

Thank you so much for the beautiful lace tablecloth
and matching placemats! They are exactly what we wanted
and will look lovely in our dining room. I'm looking forward to using them.

I can't wait to meet you at the wedding so I can thank
you in person for this considerate gift.

Sincerely,

Amy Khan

Monetary gift (example 1):

Dear Uncle Craig and Aunt Rachel,

Thank you for the generous check! We used it to purchase an antique rocking chair. It is the nicest piece of furniture that we own. We plan to slowly add other pieces as
time goes on and build our room around the chair. Please
come over soon so that you can try it out!

Lots of love,

Megan and Shawn

Monetary gift (example 2):

Dear Lisa and Wayne,

Thank you for your generous wedding gift. Nora and I have been saving for new living room furniture, and your gift has helped make that possible. It should arrive next week—we hope you'll stop by and try out our new pieces!

Thanks again. We are both looking forward to seeing you soon.

Fondly,
Jacob and Nora

Monetary gift (example 3):

Dear Grandma and Grandpa,

Thank you, thank you, thank you for such a generous wedding check! It was such a wonderful surprise. Logan and I have added it to our savings toward a new car. Thanks to you, we will be shopping for one next week. We are so grateful for this opportunity. I can't wait to stop by and take you for a spin!

Lots of love,
Mary and Logan

Monetary gift (example 4):

Dear Mr. and Mrs. Anderson,

Felicia and I appreciate your thoughtful gift. We have been looking everywhere for the perfect table to fit in our tiny kitchen. We finally found one, and your gift has made it possible for us to purchase it.

We were both glad to see you at the wedding and wish we could have spent more time together. Thanks again for your generosity.

Sincerely,

Mason and Felicia Gupta

Monetary gift (example 5):

Dear Aunt Sophie,

Nick and I really appreciate your generous gift. We plan to use it towards a new set of dinnerware. Thank you so much for your good wishes, too! We were so glad that you were able to come to the wedding. I'm looking forward to having you over for dinner next month so you can enjoy our purchase with us.

Love and best wishes,

Morgan and Nick

Musical figurines:

Dear Mrs. Alexander,

What beautiful figurines! We were delighted at the life-like detail and thrilled to discover that they were musical, too. The sound is so clear and pretty. Liam said that they were the most charming gift we received. Thank you for selecting such an exquisite gift. We will truly treasure it.

Best regards,

Mrs. Megan DuBois

Not sure what gift is (example 1):

Dear Olivia,

　　Thank you for the lovely china piece. The hand-painted flowers decorating the edges are the nicest we've ever seen. Maura and I plan to keep it on our coffee table so we can admire it often. Thank you for the time and care you must have put into your selection.

　　　　　　　　　　Fondly,
　　　　　　　　　　Ken

Not sure what gift is (example 2):

Dear Mr. and Mrs. Castillo,

　　Luis and I can't thank you enough for the beautifully carved wooden statue. It looks very exotic on our new coffee table. I know that it will receive admiring comments from everyone who visits our apartment.

　　We are so happy you will be coming to the wedding and are looking forward to seeing you there. Thanks again!

　　　　　　　　　　Best regards,
　　　　　　　　　　Jen DeLuca

Personal recipe book:

Dear Aunt Kelly,

　　Thank you so much for the book filled with all your best recipes. It was so kind of you to take the time to compile them all. Ella and I are looking forward to testing them ourselves. The next time you come to town you must stop

by for dinner. We will cook your favorite lasagna now that
you've given us your secret! Thanks again!

Love,

Evan and Ella

Returned gift to sender (annulled marriage):

Dear Mr. and Mrs. Michaels,

Jordan and I have had our marriage annulled. It is never
easy to end a marriage, but we are both better off to have
quickly discovered our mistake.

I truly liked the antique brass lamps, which are enclosed,
and I will always appreciate your kindness. Thank you.

Best regards,

Emma R. Brady

Returned gift to sender (broken engagement):

Dear Mr. and Mrs. Powell,

Kyle and I decided to call off our engagement. We are
both glad we came to this decision before the wedding took
place.

Thank you very much for the lovely decanter and set
of wine glasses, which are enclosed in this package. It was
a lovely choice and I appreciate your thoughtfulness in
selecting it.

Sincerely,

Madison Ashby

Salad serving set:

Dear Jeremy,

I'll be adding style to the simplest meal when I serve salads in this beautiful set. Thank you so much—it really is just perfect. I like the style, the size of the bowls—everything about it. I appreciate the thought and care you put into selecting this unique salad serving set. The next time you are in town, you will have to come and try it out. Thanks again!

With fond affection,
Colleen

Set of picture frames:

Dear Jill and Brendan,

We really love your gift of multiple picture frames in a variety of sizes. What a great idea! We'll have fun creating our own wall gallery. Once our pictures are framed and hanging, we'll have you over to enjoy the results.

Thank you for a really nice and thoughtful gift. We know we'll enjoy it forever.

Love and best,
Gretchen and Neil

Vintage clock:

Dear Karen,

I can't believe how well this clock suits our decor. The

vintage design, the brass pendulum—it just works perfectly. Thank you so much for this lovely and thoughtful gift.

Jeff and I appreciated your extra help on our wedding day, too. Thank you for being a good friend and for this perfect gift.

Love,
Shannon

Resources

Gift Ideas

It is customary to provide gifts to members of your wedding party as an additional way of saying thank you for participating in your celebration. The gifts do not have to be expensive; they are meant to be tokens of appreciation for your loved ones' participation in your special day. Most couples also give their parents a small gift. In addition, they exchange gifts between themselves.

This section offers some suggestions for items you might consider. There are many gifts out there specifically marketed for this purpose, but you might find just the right item on your own. Some types of gifts can be personalized with names and the wedding date—that always adds a special and memorable touch. If you have the time and talent, you can even make something yourself.

Female Attendants

Bridesmaids, Maid of Honor

These gifts are usually presented at either the bridal shower or rehearsal dinner. The maid of honor usually receives a gift that's a little different (and nicer) than the others. The reasoning: she did a lot more work and contributed more time than the other attendants. Here are some suggestions:

- Belt
- Book
- Bookmark
- Bracelet
- Charm
- Digital photo album
- Digital photo frame
- Earrings
- Flask
- Framed photo
- Handmade item
- Jewelry box
- Key ring
- Leather bag
- Lipstick case
- Locket
- Makeup
- Makeup case
- Mirror
- Music box
- Necklace
- Organizer (desk)
- Organizer (purse)
- Pendant
- Perfume
- Pin
- Pocket knife
- Purse

- Scarf
- Small tool kit
- Stationery
- Vase
- Wall hanging
- Wallet
- Watch
- Wine stopper

Flower Girl

- Bracelet
- Charm
- Framed photo
- Handmade item
- Jewelry box
- Locket
- Music box
- Necklace
- Purse
- Watch

Male Attendants

Best Man, Groomsmen, Ushers

These gifts are usually presented at the bachelor party or rehearsal dinner. The best man usually receives a special and distinctive gift. If the groom has a hobby that allows him to be creative, he can make a personal gift for each. If possible, personalizing the gift with names and the wedding date is always a nice touch. Here are some suggestions:

- Aftershave or cologne
- Belt
- Bottle opener
- Buckle
- Collar bar
- Cuff links and studs
- Digital photo album
- Digital photo frame
- Flask
- Framed photo
- Handmade item
- Key ring
- Money clip
- Organizer
- Pen set
- Personal item box
- Playing cards
- Pocket knife
- Shot glass
- Small tool kit
- Stationery
- Tie
- Tie clip
- Wallet
- Watch
- Wine stopper

Ring Bearer

- Belt
- Buckle
- Framed photo

- Handmade item
- Tie
- Tie clip
- Watch

Parents

- Album of wedding pictures
- Digital photo frame
- Digital photo album
- Flowers
- Framed photo
- Invitation from wedding engraved on beveled glass
- Necklace
- Tie tack

Your New Spouse

Exchange gifts after the wedding rehearsal. Remember, it doesn't have to be expensive. Ideally it will be something that has special meaning for both of you, something your spouse will cherish as a token of your wedding day.

For Her

- Bracelet
- Earrings
- Handmade item
- Jewelry box
- Key ring
- Locket

- Luggage
- Music box
- Pendant
- Perfume
- Pin
- Ring
- Watch

For Him

- Cologne
- Cuff links and studs
- Handmade item
- Key ring
- Luggage
- Money clip
- Music box
- Ring
- Tie bar
- Wallet
- Watch

Web Sites

Here is a collection of Web sites to help you say thank you to all your friends, family, guests, and anyone else who made your wedding memorable. I have tried to select sites that are not just lists of links but will actually help you get organized and say thank you with grace. I don't benefit in any way from these places if you use them—this list is just what I found to be the most helpful starting point for everything related to thank-yous and gift giving.

General Sites

These sites cover many wedding-related topics, including thank-you notes and gift giving.

bridalguide.com
brides.com
elegala.com
onewed.com
ourmarriage.com
theknot.com
weddingchannel.com

Wedding Web Site

These sites offer assistance and programs for creating your own wedding Web site, where you can post, among many other things, a general thank-you message (in addition to sending each person a handwritten note, of course!). Just about all the sites offer a free trial or a limited free package. Some focus on Web site design, while others offer assistance in planning, such as guest databases. Some limit the amount of data that can be imported. The best thing you can do is decide what you need and select the one that most suits those needs.

ewedding.com
ourweddingplus.com
wedpagedesigns.com
wedsimple.com
wedshare.com
weddingwindow.com

Databases
see also Wedding Web Sites

bridaltrack.com

Favors and Other Gifts

americanbridal.com

charmingweddings.com

efavors.com

Rings

loveweddingbands.com

weddingrings.com

Invitations and Stationers

beautifulweddinginvitations.com

crane.com

dauphinepress.com

finestationery.com

formal-invitations.com

invitationsbydawn.com

myexpression.com

mygatsby.com

rexcraft.com

theamericanwedding.com

wedding-needs.com

weddingpaperdivas.com

Registry

myregistry.com

Index

acknowledgment cards, 4,11,16
address, 3, 8–9, 14–16, 26–27,
    33–35, 41, 45, 49
annulment, 37
attendants, vii, 77–79

best man, 41, 44, 79
binder, 14
bridal shower, 77
bridesmaid, 9, 41, 44, 55, 77
broken engagement, 60, 74
broken gift, 59, 62

cake stand, 59, 62
centerpiece bowl, 59, 63
ceramic vase, 60, 69
champagne, 59, 63, 64
computer, 4, 11, 14
consultant, 42, 57
crystal vase, 28, 59, 65

database, 15
descriptive phrases, 29
descriptive words, 28

digital photo album, 59, 65–66,
    78, 80–81
digital photo frame, 78, 80–81
duplicate gifts, 5, 34

e-mail, vi, 3, 10, 14
engraved, 5, 21, 81
etiquette, vii, 17–18, 36
    amount of time guest has
        to send gift, 36
    amount of time couple has
        to send notes, 8
    notes sent before the
        wedding, 3–4, 8–9,
        18–21, 33

flower girl, 9, 41, 46–47, 79
flowers, 47, 65, 67, 73, 81
framed photo, 78–81

gift
    amount of time guest has
        to send, 36
    broken, 59, 62

don't know giver of, 5, 35
duplicate, 5, 34
exchanged, 59, 66
group, 5, 13, 34, 59, 60,
    67–68
ideas for attendants', vii,
    77–79
ideas for parents', 41, 77,
    81
ideas for spouse's, vii, 81
monetary, vi, 5, 34–35, 60,
    70–72
never received, 5, 37
not sure what it is, 60, 73
returned to sender, 60, 74
gift basket, 59, 67
gift card, 59, 67
gift without a card, 5, 35
groomsman, 41, 47
groomsmen, 44, 79
group gift, 5, 13, 34, 59, 60,
    67–68
guest(s), vi, 9–11, 14–16, 30,
    34, 36, 41, 47–48, 55–56,
    65

hand-carved napkin rings, 60,
    68
handmade quilt, 60, 69
handwritten note, 10–11
hosted wedding guests, 41, 48

index cards, 13

list of sample letters
    gifts received, vii, 39, 59,
        61
    those who helped, vii, 39,
        41, 43
list of questions, 3–5

maid of honor, 48–49, 77
mailing notes, 3, 9–10
monetary gift, vi, 5, 34–35, 60,
    70–72
monograms, 4, 18, 20
music, 41, 49, 78–79, 82

name,
    after the wedding, 3–4,
        7–8, 18–21, 33
    before the wedding, 3–4,
        7–8, 18–21, 33
    maiden, 4, 8, 18–19, 33
new address, 41, 49
notes,
    amount of time couple has
        to send, 8
officiant, 41, 50
organizing,
    binder, 14
    database, 15

forgetting someone, 15–16
index cards, 13–15
saving time when, 3, 8, 18

paper, 4, 11, 17
parents, 9, 15, 35, 41, 50–51, 77, 81
party, 9, 15, 35, 41–42, 44–45, 46, 51–52, 54, 77, 79
phone, thanking someone via, vi
photo, framed, 78–81
preprinted verses, vi, 3–4, 10–11, 13, 16–17

reader at ceremony, 42, 52
recipe book, 60, 73
rehearsal dinner, 42, 52, 77, 79
return address, 3, 9
returned gift to sender, 37, 60, 74
ring bearer, 9, 42, 53, 80
rules, vii, 17

salad serving set, 60, 75
sample letters, vii, 37, 41–76
set of picture frames, 60, 75
shower, vi, 9, 14–15, 37, 42, 48, 53–54, 77
signing the note, 3–5, 7–8, 11, 19, 31, 33

social networking site, vi
special favor, 14, 42, 55
spouse, vii, 20, 26–27, 35, 81
stationery, 4, 17–18, 20–21, 79–80

table linens, 60, 70
text messages, vi, 3, 10–11

usher, 9, 42, 55, 79
unsigned card, 5, 35

videographer, 42, 56
vintage clock, 60, 75
vocalist, 42, 56

wedding Web site, vi, 3, 10, 36
writing the note
    addressee concerns, 26–27, 31, 33–34
    basic structure for, 26
    descriptive phrases, 29
    descriptive words, 28
    ink color, 25
    names, 26–27, 33
    signing off, 26, 31
    tell the person how you might use the gift, 26, 29–30
    ways to begin, 26–27
    ways to say thanks, 27, 31

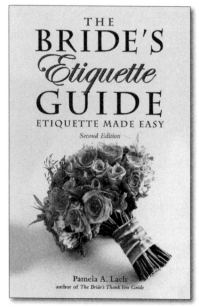